Exploring
CALIFORNIA
MISSIONS

CENTRAL COAST MISSIONS IN CALIFORNIA

❖

BY
JUNE BEHRENS

❖

CONSULTANT:
JAMES J. RAWLS, PH.D.
PROFESSOR EMERITUS
DEPARTMENT OF HISTORY
DIABLO VALLEY COLLEGE

LERNER PUBLICATIONS COMPANY/MINNEAPOLIS

The images in this book were used with the permission of: © North Wind Picture Archives, pp. 6, 16, 23, 43, 55; © Digital Vision/Getty Images, p. 8; © Marilyn "Angel" Wynn/Nativestock.com, pp. 10, 12; San Diego Museum of Man, p. 13; © Lake County Museum/CORBIS, p. 15; Zephyrin Engelhardt, *The Missions and Missionaries of California*, 1908-1915, pp. 17, 21, 29, 35, 44, 47; © age fotostock/SuperStock, pp. 18, 52; © Eda Rogers, pp. 24, 56; © SuperStock, Inc./SuperStock, p. 27; © Richard Cummins/CORBIS, p. 31; Library of Congress, p. 32 (HABS CAL,42-LOMP.V,1); © Tom Brakefield/SuperStock, pp. 33, 45; © Richard Cummins/SuperStock, pp. 37, 38, 53, 54; © Historic Urban Plans, p. 40; Courtesy of the Bancroft Library, University of California, Berkley, p. 48; Seaver Center for Western History, Los Angeles County Museum of Natural History, p. 50; AP Photo/Mark J. Terrill, p. 57. Illustrations on pp. 4, 11, 23, 58, 59 by © Laura Westlund/Independent Picture Service.

Front cover: © John Elk III.
Back cover: © Laura Westlund/Independent Picture Service.

Lerner Publications Company
A division of Lerner Publishing Group, Inc.
241 First Avenue North
Minneapolis, MN 55401 U.S.A.

Website address: www.lernerbooks.com

Library of Congress Cataloging-in-Publication Data

Behrens, June.
    Central coast missions in California / by June Behrens.
        p.   cm. —   (Exploring California missions)
    Includes index.
    ISBN-13: 978-0-8225-0897-7 (lib. bdg. : alk. paper)
    1. Missions, Spanish—California—Pacific Coast—History—Juvenile literature. 2. Pacific Coast (Calif.)—History, Local—Juvenile literature. 3. Santa Barbara Mission—History—Juvenile literature. 4. Mission La Purísima Concepción (Calif.)—History—Juvenile literature. 5. Santa Inés Mission (Solvang, Calif.)—History—Juvenile literature. 6. Spanish mission buildings—California—Pacific Coast—Juvenile literature. 7. Chumash Indians—Missions—California—Pacific Coast—History—Juvenile literature. 8. California—History—To 1846—Juvenile literature. I. Title.
F868.P33B44 2008
979.4'9—dc22   2006036848

Manufactured in the United States of America
1 2 3 4 5 6 – DP – 13 12 11 10 09 08

CONTENTS

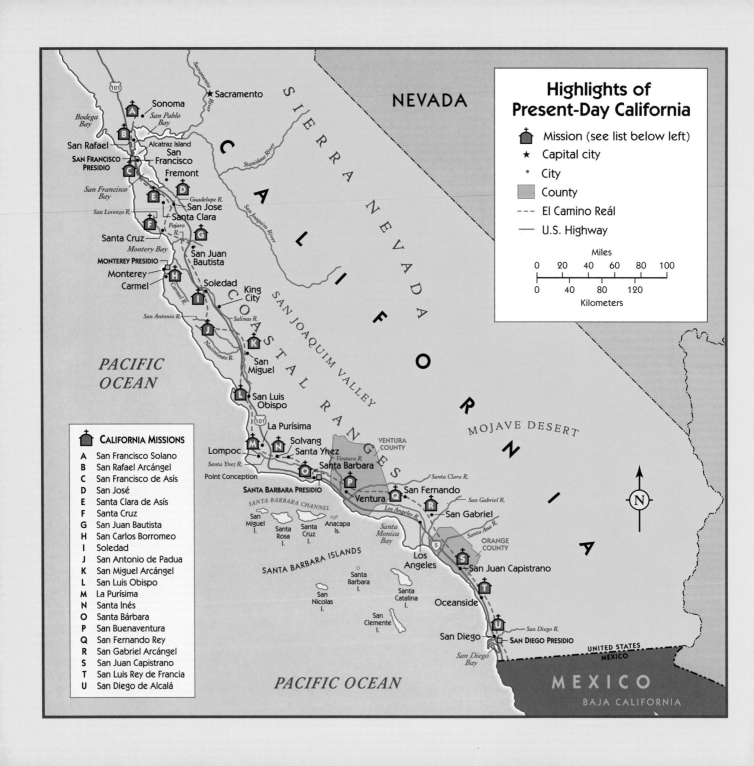

Highlights of Present-Day California

- ⛪ Mission (see list below left)
- ★ Capital city
- • City
- County
- --- El Camino Reál
- — U.S. Highway

Miles
0 20 40 60 80 100

0 40 80 120
Kilometers

⛪ CALIFORNIA MISSIONS

A   San Francisco Solano
B   San Rafael Arcángel
C   San Francisco de Asís
D   San José
E   Santa Clara de Asís
F   Santa Cruz
G   San Juan Bautista
H   San Carlos Borromeo
I   Soledad
J   San Antonio de Padua
K   San Miguel Arcángel
L   San Luis Obispo
M   La Purísima
N   Santa Inés
O   Santa Bárbara
P   San Buenaventura
Q   San Fernando Rey
R   San Gabriel Arcángel
S   San Juan Capistrano
T   San Luis Rey de Francia
U   San Diego de Alcalá

NEVADA

CALIFORNIA

SIERRA NEVADA

COASTAL RANGES

SAN JOAQUIM VALLEY

MOJAVE DESERT

PACIFIC OCEAN

PACIFIC OCEAN

MEXICO
BAJA CALIFORNIA

UNITED STATES
MEXICO

Sacramento River
Stanislaus River
San Joaquin River
Guadelupe R.
San Lorenzo R.
Pajaro R.
Carmel R.
San Antonio R.
Salinas R.
Nacimiento R.
Santa Ynez R.
Ventura R.
Santa Clara R.
San Gabriel R.
Santa Ana R.
Los Angeles R.
San Diego R.

Bodega Bay
San Pablo Bay
San Francisco Bay
Monterey Bay
Santa Monica Bay
Santa Barbara Channel
San Diego Bay

★ Sacramento
Sonoma
San Rafael
SAN FRANCISCO PRESIDIO
Alcatraz Island
San Francisco
Fremont
San Jose
Santa Clara
Santa Cruz
San Juan Bautista
MONTEREY PRESIDIO
Monterey
Carmel
Soledad
King City
San Miguel
San Luis Obispo
La Purísima
Lompoc
Solvang
Santa Ynez
Santa Barbara
Point Conception
SANTA BARBARA PRESIDIO
Ventura
San Fernando
San Gabriel
Los Angeles
ORANGE COUNTY
VENTURA COUNTY
San Juan Capistrano
Oceanside
San Diego
SAN DIEGO PRESIDIO

SANTA BARBARA ISLANDS
San Miguel I.
Santa Rosa I.
Santa Cruz I.
Anacapa Is.
San Nicolas I.
Santa Barbara I.
Santa Catalina I.
San Clemente I.

N

INTRODUCTION

Spain and the Roman Catholic Church built twenty California **missions** between 1769 and 1817. A final mission was built in 1823. The missions stand along a narrow strip of California's Pacific coast. Today, the missions sit near Highway 101. They are between the cities of San Diego and Sonoma.

The Spaniards built **presidios** (forts) and missions throughout their empire. This system helped the Spanish claim and protect new lands. In California, the main goal of the mission system was to control Native Americans and their lands. The Spaniards wanted Native Americans to accept their leadership and way of life.

Spanish **missionaries** and soldiers ran the presidio and mission system. Father Junípero Serra was the missions' first leader. He was called father-president. Father Serra and the other priests taught Native Americans the Catholic faith. The priests showed them how to behave like Spaniards. The soldiers made sure Native Americans obeyed the priests.

The area was home to many Native American groups. They had their own beliefs and practices. The Spanish ways were much different from their own. Some Native Americans willingly joined the missions. But others did not. They did not want to give up their own ways of life.

The Spaniards tried different methods to make Native Americans join their missions. Sometimes they gave the Native Americans gifts. Other times, the Spanish used force. To stay alive, the Native Americans had no choice but to join the missions.

The Spanish called Native Americans who joined their missions **neophytes.** The Spaniards taught neophytes the Catholic religion. The neophytes built buildings and farmed the land. They also produced goods, such as cloth and soap. They built a trade route connecting the missions. It was called El Camino Reál (the Royal Road). The goods and trade were expected to earn money and power for Spain.

Spanish missionary Father Garzes instructs Native Americans.

But the system did not last. More than half of the Native Americans died from diseases the Spaniards brought. Mexico took control of the area in 1821 and closed the missions. Neophytes were free to leave or stay at the missions. In 1848, the United States gained control of California. Some of the remaining neophytes returned to their people. But many others had no people to return to. They moved to **pueblos** (towns) or inland areas. The missions sat empty. They fell apart over time.

This book is about three missions that sit along the coast of central California. Mission Santa Bárbara Virgen y Mártir was the tenth mission in California. It was founded in 1786. The eleventh mission, La Purísima Concepción de Maria Santísima, followed in 1787. Years later, in 1804, Santa Inés Virgen y Mártir was built between Santa Bárbara and La Purísima.

CALIFORNIA MISSION	FOUNDING DATE
San Diego de Alcalá	July 16, 1769
San Carlos Borromeo de Carmelo	June 3, 1770
San Antonio de Padua	July 14, 1771
San Gabriel Arcángel	September 8, 1771
San Luis Obispo de Tolosa	September 1, 1772
San Francisco de Asís	June 29, 1776
San Juan Capistrano	November 1, 1776
Santa Clara de Asís	January 12, 1777
San Buenaventura	March 31, 1782
Santa Bárbara Virgen y Mártir	December 4, 1786
La Purísima Concepción de Maria Santísima	December 8, 1787
Santa Cruz	August 28, 1791
Nuestra Señora de la Soledad	October 9, 1791
San José	June 11, 1797
San Juan Bautista	June 24, 1797
San Miguel Arcángel	July 25, 1797
San Fernando Rey de España	September 8, 1797
San Luis Rey de Francia	June 13, 1798
Santa Inés Virgen y Mártir	September 17, 1804
San Rafael Arcángel	December 14, 1817
San Francisco Solano	July 4, 1823

The rugged central
coast of California

❖ 1 ❖

EARLY LIFE ALONG THE COAST

On California's central coast, rocky cliffs towered over the pounding surf. Dolphins and whales leaped and dove among the waves. Hungry birds swooped low to catch fish and shellfish.

Inland from the coast, grassy river valleys wound through rolling hills. Rabbits, squirrels, and other small animals darted among oak and maple trees. The Santa Ynez River ran through the valleys. Rugged mountains lay far in the distance.

The Chumash bent branches to create dome huts. They then covered the domes with bundles of grass.

For thousands of years, people shared this land with nature. The Chumash Indians were the first group to live in the central coast area. They were also the largest group. Most of their villages stood along the coast or near rivers.

DAILY LIFE

Like all Native Americans, the Chumash lived off the land. They built dome-shaped houses from young trees and long, stiff grasses. They ate animals, seeds, and plants.

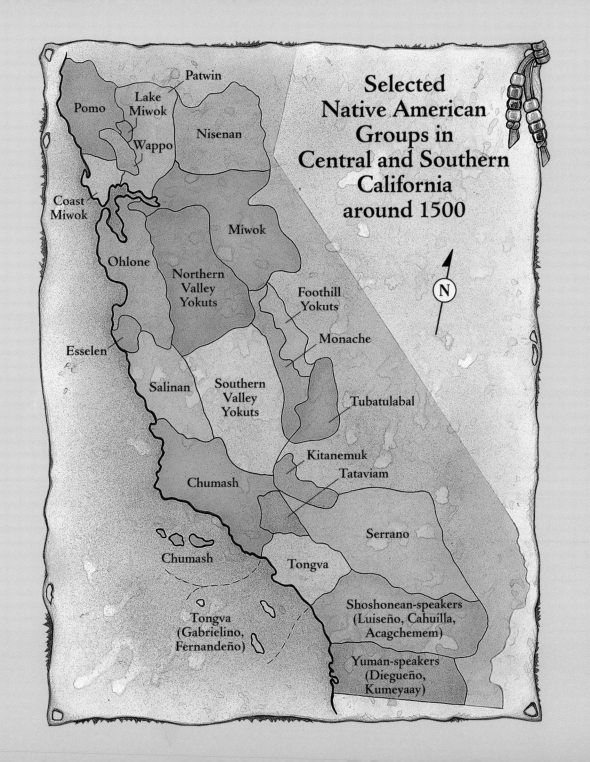

Selected
Native American
Groups in
Central and Southern
California
around 1500

N

Patwin
Lake Miwok
Pomo
Wappo
Nisenan
Coast Miwok
Miwok
Ohlone
Northern Valley Yokuts
Foothill Yokuts
Monache
Esselen
Salinan
Southern Valley Yokuts
Tubatulabal
Kitanemuk
Tataviam
Chumash
Serrano
Chumash
Tongva
Tongva (Gabrielino, Fernandeño)
Shoshonean-speakers (Luiseño, Cahuilla, Acagchemem)
Yuman-speakers (Diegueño, Kumeyaay)

But most of their food came from the ocean. Meals often included fish, shellfish, and seaweed.

Chumash women did most of the cooking. They also cared for the children. The women collected plants for both food and medicine. They gathered shellfish close to shore. They used rocks to grind acorns into flour. The men built strong canoes

Chumash women grind acorns and water into a nutritious mush.

Religious leaders used rattles made of deer hooves in religious celebrations.

for fishing. They hunted with bows and arrows. The Chumash did not grow crops. The food they ate grew naturally.

Each village had artists who made shell jewelry, wooden bowls, and reed baskets. A chief handled village business. A religious leader, called a shaman, healed the sick. The shaman also spoke with the Chumash gods.

Religion was important to the Chumash. They believed that every living thing was holy. During religious services, they sang and danced to honor nature. They gave thanks every day by caring for the land that gave them so much.

STRANGERS ARRIVE

In 1542, a Spanish explorer named Juan Rodríguez Cabrillo sailed north from **New Spain**. (This area later became Mexico.) Cabrillo was exploring the coast. The Spaniards called this land California. The Chumash greeted Cabrillo and his crew with gifts of food and water. The Spaniards gave the Native Americans glass beads and other gifts in return. Cabrillo claimed California for Spain, even though the Chumash were already living there. In 1602, Spain sent another explorer. His name was Sebastián Vizcaíno. Then, for about 160 years, Spain seemed to forget about California.

As time went on, the king of Spain got nervous. He worried that another country might try to take away the land called California. He sent Captain Gaspar de Portolá and a group of soldiers there. They were to set up presidios. These forts would protect the Spaniards from attack. A Catholic priest named Father Junípero Serra went with them. He set up missions. The missions would help spread the Catholic faith.

THE MISSION SYSTEM

Father Serra founded the first California mission in 1769. He named it San Diego de Alcalá. He chose two priests to run the mission. Then he left to establish more missions along the California coast.

The main job of the missions was to teach the Catholic faith to the Native Americans. The Spaniards wanted to have as many people as possible join their faith. They also wanted Native Americans to become loyal to Spain and to become neophytes at the missions. Having many Spanish missions and towns in the area would show that the land belonged to Spain.

Father Junípero Serra walked across much of California to found missions.

For the missions to succeed, neophytes would have to grow food. They would also have to make most of the goods the missions needed. The Spanish government would help. It would provide soldiers and some money. The government would also send a few supplies that the neophytes could not make themselves.

Spanish officials figured that it would take ten years to train the neophytes. Then they could run the mission by themselves. When that time came, the Catholic Church would turn the land over to the neophytes. Only the mission church would be run by the priests. The neophytes would farm the land. And they would pay taxes to Spain. The priests would go off to start new missions.

Some neophytes chose to adopt the Spanish faith and style of clothing.

Neophytes ran the farms at the missions.

The priests believed that the mission system would help the Chumash learn a better way of life. They did not understand that the Native Americans had a right to live the way they wanted to.

Mission Santa Bárbara is called Queen of the Missions because it is so beautiful.

2

MISSIONS OF THE CENTRAL COAST

The stories of missions Santa Bárbara, La Purísima, and Santa Inés are very much alike. Each was about one day's journey from the next. The three missions were protected by the same presidio. It was at Santa Barbara. The area contained many large Chumash villages. The Santa Ynez River supplied water. Each site had many trees for building the missions. The soil was good for farming. Father Serra and the rest of the Spaniards thought that setting up these missions would be easy.

But they were wrong. The Chumash liked their way of life. They would not give it up without a fight.

MISSION SANTA BÁRBARA

In the early 1780s, Father Serra chose the site for Mission Santa Bárbara Virgen y Mártir. But his plans for the mission had to wait until a presidio was built. Before the presidio was finished, Father Serra died. Father Fermín Francisco de Lasuén took over as father-president of the mission system.

On December 4, 1786, Father Lasuén blessed the site for California's tenth mission. Twelve days later, the governor of New Spain arrived for the official founding of Santa Bárbara.

Some Chumash Indians helped build a simple, wooden chapel and living quarters. The priests encouraged the workers to be baptized. In a baptism ceremony, priests used water to bless people and to welcome them as new members of the Christian faith. The Chumash didn't speak Spanish.

And they probably didn't understand what baptism meant. Some Chumash agreed to the ceremony. But they may have been attracted by the church music or by baptism gifts of blankets and clothing. Most Chumash in the area chose not to join the mission.

A priest baptizes a Native American baby, welcoming it into the Christian faith.

To help convince them, the priests at Santa Bárbara offered them a plam. The Chumash could continue to live in their villages. They were to come to the mission every day. They worked and went to church services. In return, they received clothes, food, and other goods. This plan made the mission an easier choice for the Chumash. Santa Bárbara began to grow.

MISSION LIFE

Once neophytes were baptized, they were expected to eat, dress, and worship as the Spaniards did. The men learned how to farm the land and raise animals. They built Spanish-style buildings. Women learned to spin wool into yarn and to weave cloth. The Spaniards taught them to make candles and soap. They also learned to cook Spanish foods.

Every morning, the priests rang a bell at sunrise. The bell called everyone to church. Then people ate breakfast and started the day's work. At noon, the neophytes stopped for lunch. They took a siesta, or rest break. Then they returned to work. Children attended morning and afternoon classes.

Neophyte workers made rope for the mission to use or sell.

A bell rang again at five for the evening church service. Supper was served afterward. Many of the neophytes at Santa Bárbara returned to their villages for the night. But those who lived at the mission were even told when to go to bed. For women, bedtime was eight. Men could stay up until nine.

Such a strict schedule was new to the neophytes. They were used to working and sleeping when they wanted. But their hard work produced big results.

SUCCESS AT SANTA BÁRBARA

By 1787, Santa Bárbara had grown. It included a kitchen and storerooms. These buildings were made of **adobe**, a kind of clay. The clay was mixed with straw and water. Then it was formed into bricks. The bricks dried in the sun. Then the hard bricks were used to build strong, thick walls. In 1789, the growing mission replaced the original, wooden church with a larger, adobe church. Just five years later, they moved to an even larger one.

Adobe bricks remain in the old mission walls. Neophytes used rectangular molds to shape the bricks.

The main mission buildings were built close to one another. Together, the buildings formed the sides of a rectangle. There was an open area in the middle. This building plan is called a **quadrangle**. Outside the quadrangle, workers built small adobe homes. Neophyte families lived in them. Beyond the mission's buildings lay its fields and pastures.

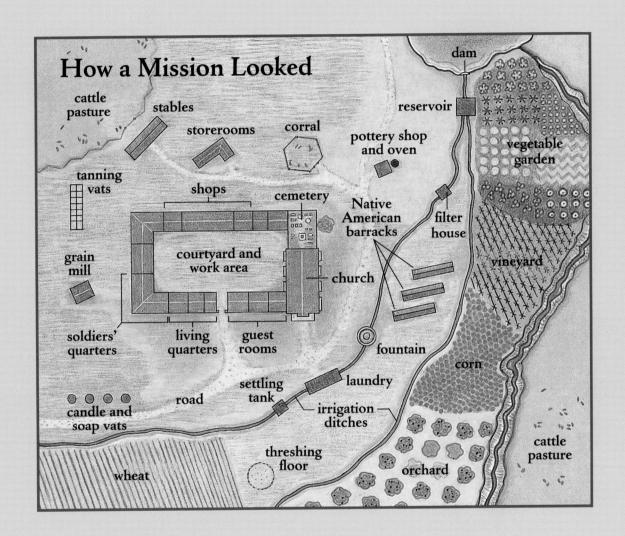

How a Mission Looked

cattle pasture

stables

storerooms

corral

pottery shop and oven

dam

reservoir

vegetable garden

tanning vats

shops

cemetery

Native American barracks

filter house

vineyard

grain mill

courtyard and work area

church

soldiers' quarters

living quarters

guest rooms

fountain

corn

candle and soap vats

road

settling tank

laundry

irrigation ditches

threshing floor

orchard

cattle pasture

wheat

As Santa Bárbara grew, it took over more and more land. For hundreds of years, the Chumash had used this land for hunting and gathering food. Instead, workers planted crops or grazed animals there. Many Chumash couldn't find enough to eat. They had two choices. They could move inland or join the mission.

In 1801, a terrible sickness spread through the mission. Illnesses like this were common throughout California. Spaniards accidentally spread diseases to the Native Americans. These diseases were new to the Chumash. Their bodies could not fight the diseases. Thousands of people died.

The neophytes around Santa Bárbara were frightened. They tried to undo their baptism ceremonies. They held religious ceremonies from their own culture. The priests were angry. They made stricter rules. They forced the neophytes to move to the mission.

The next years were busy at Santa Bárbara. Neophytes built a system of ditches. The ditches carried water from a nearby creek. The people used the water for growing crops, washing clothes, and cooking. Large pools stored water for times when the creek ran low. Mission workers cared for vineyards and orchards. Workers also raised a large herd of sheep.

In 1812, a large earthquake destroyed the mission's church. Three years later, work began on a new church. This one was made of stone. It had six columns on the front. It also had a large bell tower. The beautiful church was finished in 1820. It earned Santa Bárbara the name Queen of the Missions.

The new church at Mission Santa Bárbara was made of white stone. A second bell tower was added in 1831.

By 1823, nearly one thousand neophytes were living at Santa Bárbara. The mission sold wine and fruit to earn money. It also sold fine wool blankets and cloth.

THE NEOPHYTES FIGHT BACK

From the outside, Santa Bárbara looked as if it were successful. But inside, things were not going so well. The neophytes were unhappy. They did not like the strict rules. And they were frightened by the sickness around them. Many of them ran away. Neophytes who got caught were beaten or locked up.

Runaways were a big problem at Santa Bárbara. The priests needed to do something. They decided to let the neophytes invite friends and families to visit them at the mission. But such a small favor was not enough. Neophytes at Santa Inés and La Purísima were angry too.

In 1824, trouble broke out between neophytes and soldiers. At Santa Bárbara, an *alcalde*, or Chumash manager, was in charge of the neophytes. This man was named Andrés Sagimomatsse. He and other Chumash attacked the soldiers at the mission. Three Chumash died. Others were forced to flee. For weeks, the men hid in the nearby hills. Eventually, many of them returned to the mission.

The relationship between the priests and the neophytes at Santa Bárbara would never be the same. Over the next ten years, the mission's population dropped below five hundred.

Spanish soldiers fight neophytes within sight of Mission Santa Bárbara during the revolt of 1824.

MISSION LA PURÍSIMA CONCEPCIÓN

On December 8, 1787, Father Lasuén founded the eleventh California mission, La Purísima Concepción de Maria Santísima. But work on the new mission had to wait until the rainy season ended. Then the soil had to dry out. Soldiers arrived to begin clearing land. They began building the mission. Workers from Santa Bárbara came to help.

In the first few months, priests at La Purísima baptized seventy-five people. The neophytes helped to build buildings and plant crops. But the priests did not force them to follow a strict schedule. People could come and go as they wished. Later, as the number of neophytes grew, the priests set stricter rules.

In 1789, workers finished an adobe church. This building formed one side of La Purísima's quadrangle. Living quarters, workshops, and storage buildings made up the other three sides. Outside the quadrangle, a large herd of cattle grazed.

This statue of Father Fermín de Lasuén watches over a garden in one of his missions.

By 1798, the mission was home to more than nine hundred neophytes. The church could not hold them all. Workers began to build a bigger one. The work was finished in 1802.

By 1804, 1,520 neophytes lived at La Purísima. That same year, a new priest arrived at the mission. His name was Father Mariano Payeras. He oversaw the construction of ditches. The ditches carried water from the river to the mission and its fields. The priest also began to trade with Spanish settlers. But La Purísima's success wouldn't last.

Only ruins remain of the first adobe church at Mission La Purísima.

DISASTER STRIKES

The first disaster to hit La Purísima was sickness. Between 1804 and 1807, one-third of the neophytes died. Others were afraid and ran away.

Then, in December 1812, a large earthquake left huge cracks in the ground around the mission. The quake was followed by several months of heavy rain. The mission buildings began to fall apart.

In 1813, the priests decided to rebuild the mission at a new site about four miles away. This time, workers arranged the buildings in a line rather than in a quadrangle. This way, people could get out quickly in case of another earthquake. Workers used rock to make the walls thicker and stronger than before. They built more workshops, a hospital, and a fountain. La Purísima was on its feet again. By 1815, the number of neophytes had risen to one thousand.

A covered walkway shades the doors to the priests' quarters at the new Mission La Purísima.

The next disaster to strike was a **drought**. For several years, little rain fell. Crops failed, and livestock died. The dry conditions led to a fire in 1818. It destroyed the neophytes' living quarters. Then, in 1823, Father Payeras died. The mission mourned its popular leader.

FIGHTING AT THE MISSIONS

During these hard times, the Spanish government was busy fighting a war with the people of New Spain. The government stopped sending money and supplies to California. It also stopped paying the soldiers. The soldiers were angry. They took out their anger on the neophytes. This made life even tougher for the neophytes. They faced more harsh treatment from the soldiers. And the neophytes still had to take care of the cruel men. The soldiers had no money to buy food and clothing. The neophytes had to cook the soldiers' meals and sew their clothes.

Trouble broke out in 1824. A neophyte visiting Santa Inés from La Purísima was beaten by a soldier. Angry neophytes at Santa Inés fought back. The people at La Purísima heard the

The neophytes fought hard against the Spanish soldiers, who had more guns and ammunition.

news. They began their own **revolt**, or attack, against the Spaniards. The neophytes at La Purísima took control of the mission. They built a wall in front of the church. They shot cannons to keep soldiers away. The neophytes kept control of the mission for nearly a month. Then an army of 109 soldiers arrived at the mission. They broke through the wall. The soldiers attacked the neophytes. In three hours, sixteen Native Americans and one soldier were killed. Many others were hurt.

As punishment for the revolt, soldiers killed seven neophytes. And they sent twelve others to prison. The priests tried to renew the neophytes' trust in the mission. But it was too late. Many people left.

❖❖❖

MISSION SANTA INÉS

The third central coast mission was founded on September 17, 1804. Father Lasuén had died in 1803. The new head of the missions was Father Estéban Tápis. He blessed the site for Mission Santa Inés Virgen y Mártir.

By this time, California had eighteen other missions. Santa Inés was located halfway between Santa Bárbara and La Purísima. These neighbors sent neophytes to live and work at the new mission. Within three months, they built a church, priests' quarters, and storerooms. During that time, priests baptized 112 Chumash.

Soon Santa Inés was getting crowded. Builders worked as fast as they could. By 1806, the quadrangle was completed. The mission's farming and ranching operations were booming. The neophytes became well known for their fine saddles and other leather goods.

A SETBACK

The 1812 earthquake dealt a severe blow to Santa Inés. The

At first, the neophytes struggled to make Mission Santa Inés big enough for everyone who wanted to live there.

church was destroyed. Many other buildings were damaged. The neophytes set to work making repairs. And they built a temporary church. Construction of a bigger, stronger church began in 1814 and ended in 1817. The new building had thick walls of adobe and brick.

That same year, the population of Santa Inés peaked at 920 neophytes. Some of them worked to replace the old water system with underground pipes. Others tended the mission's twelve thousand animals and acres of farmland. Talented artists created beautiful paintings called **murals** on the walls of the new church.

UNREST

The neophytes at Santa Inés had a beautiful home. And they had plenty of food. Still, they were unhappy. Like neophytes at the other missions, they ate the same foods every day. For breakfast and supper, they had a kind of porridge called *atole*. For lunch, they ate a meat stew called posole. They

Bells for the new church were ordered from Lima, Peru.

were told when to wake up, work, and sleep. If they broke the rules (and sometimes even if they didn't), the soldiers punished them.

Then, in 1824, one of the soldiers whipped a visiting neophyte. A thousand angry Chumash fought back. They locked up the priests. They attacked the soldiers. And they set fire to the church. The battle lasted until the next day. Then soldiers arrived from Santa Bárbara. Two Chumash Indians died in the fighting.

After the revolt, many neophytes ran away. Without workers, the mission began to crumble.

The town of Santa Barbara grew bigger along carefully planned streets.

STATE CONTROL OF THE MISSIONS

The neophytes weren't the only people fighting for their freedom. In 1810, the people of New Spain went to war against Spain. In 1821, they won their independence. They called their new country the Republic of Mexico. California and its valuable missions had belonged to Spain. When Spain lost the war, the Mexican government took control of California.

The new Mexican government needed to protect its claim to California. Mexican leaders urged people to move there. They wanted the settlers to start farms and ranches.

The settlers were called **Californios**. They complained bitterly to the government that the missions had already taken the best land.

In the 1830s, the Mexican government began to pass laws to take the mission lands away from the Catholic Church. This process was called **secularization**. The government replaced the Spanish missionaries with Mexican priests. The new priests held services. But they no longer worked to attract new people to Christianity. Neophytes were free to leave.

Government leaders hired people to divide the missions' property. They were called civil administrators. The civil administrators were supposed to give some of the land to neophytes and to sell the rest. But most of the administrators were greedy. They took the best land for themselves and for their friends and family. Few of the neophytes received anything. Most of those who did receive land did not own it for long. Californios tricked many Native Americans into selling their valuable land at cheap prices.

Even without land of their own, some neophytes were glad to be free. But many of them had no money. And they had

A few neophyte families were able to buy oxcarts and start ranches of their own.

nowhere to go. They had never learned to live off the land, as their parents or grandparents had. Their families' villages had been wiped out by disease. Some people moved away to join other Native American communities. Others took jobs on ranches in exchange for food, shelter, and clothing.

SECULARIZATION ALONG
THE CENTRAL COAST

Mexico secularized the three central coast missions in 1834. The priests at Santa Bárbara were allowed to keep their church. They also kept the cemetery and their living quarters. The government sold the rest of the land to Californios. The neophytes received nothing. By 1839, only

Priests and ex-neophytes welcome Bishop García Diego y Moreno *(center)* to Santa Bárbara.

After Mission La Purísima *(right)* was secularized, its priests moved to Mission Santa Inés.

246 neophytes were left. The mission was falling apart. In 1842, a high-ranking church official came to Santa Bárbara. His name was Bishop García Diego y Moreno. He used the church buildings as his headquarters.

Conditions were worse at La Purísima. The administrator in charge of the mission stole property. He also mistreated the neophytes. Soon the priests left. Then the neophytes followed. The buildings soon fell down. In 1845, the Mexican government finally sold the mission for $1,110.

When Santa Inés was secularized, it was the richest mission in California. But the Mexican government did not care to run it. It sold the livestock. Then it rented most of the buildings to a Mexican family. The priests stayed. They lived in the church. But the remaining neophytes had to leave. In the early 1840s, Bishop Diego y Moreno used the mission as a school for priests.

In 1846, Bishop Diego y Moreno died. The Catholic Church sold his headquarters at Santa Bárbara. Later that year, two Californios bought the property at Santa Inés. They paid seven thousand dollars for it. But before the men could take control of the land, Mexico went to war with theUnited States.

THE UNITED STATES TAKES OVER

Mexico had long argued with the United States over its **borders**. In 1846, the U.S. government declared war on Mexico. Fighting took place throughout Mexico, including several battles in California. By 1848, the war was over. Mexico lost control of about half of its lands. On

September 9, 1850, the United States made California its thirty-first state.

Meanwhile, thousands of people began to pour into California. Miners had discovered gold. Everyone wanted to get rich. People scrambled to buy land. Californios and other white landowners went to court. They had to prove ownership of their property. Many didn't have the right papers, so they lost their land.

Soldiers raise the U.S. flag after capturing the Mexican presidio at Monterey.

The situation was even worse for Native American landowners. Settlers simply forced them off their land. The laws of the United States did not protect the Native Americans' rights to own property. They had no way to fight back in court. Even those who had been lucky enough to receive mission lands had nowhere to go.

Many Native Americans in California were forced by the government to relocate to lower-quality farmland.

The government began to set aside special areas just for Native Americans. These areas were called **reservations**. But they were no good for farming. Some American Indians moved there. But many were unable to grow food or make a living. They had to depend on the government for food and money. In the central coast area, the government established a reservation for Chumash Indians near Mission Santa Inés.

The old mission buildings were returned to the Catholic Church. Most of the buildings had been damaged by thieves, weather, and lack of care. And the U.S. government did not have a use for churches, no matter what condition they were in. The Catholic Church wanted to use the buildings. But it had little money for repairs.

Artist Edward Deakin painted
this crumbling wing of
Mission Bárbara.

·4·

THE MISSIONS IN MODERN TIMES

For many years, people forgot about the missions. Then, in 1884, Helen Hunt Jackson wrote a book about Native Americans during and after mission times. The book was meant to encourage better treatment of Native Americans.

Most readers ignored that part of the story. They saw mission life as an exciting adventure. They wanted to visit the historic sites. Soon a group of history lovers formed the Landmarks Club. They started to raise money to **restore**, or fix up, the missions.

SANTA BÁRBARA

Mission Santa Bárbara survived secularization fairly well. The Catholic Church had taken care of the buildings. It ran a religious school there. Tourists began to visit in the late 1800s. The beautiful church and other buildings were still standing. But in 1925, a huge earthquake knocked down one of the bell towers. The other tower cracked. Other buildings were also damaged. After the earthquake, people gave $400,000 to help restore Santa Bárbara. But by 1950, even the restored buildings were falling apart. Workers tore down the front of the mission and the bell towers. Then they rebuilt them.

Thousands of visitors tour Mission Santa Bárbara every year.

The restored mission holds a museum and library. Priests still live at the mission. They hold services there every day. Each May, the mission hosts an art festival. It is called I Madonnari. Artists decorate the streets in front of the mission with colorful chalk drawings of the Madonna (the mother of Jesus).

The Saint Barbara Parish holds weekly services in the Mission Santa Bárbara church.

SANTA INÉS

Mission Santa Inés was restored more slowly. In 1882, the Donahue family moved into the priests' quarters. They worked hard to keep up with repairs. Finally, after sixteen years, they gave up and moved away. In 1904, a priest took up the project. His name was Father Alexander Buckler. In twenty years, he restored about one-fourth of the quadrangle. He also repaired mission artwork and religious items. More repairs were made between 1947 and 1954.

This statue of Saint Inés stands in the chapel at Mission Santa Inés.

The mission received much care over the years. Some of the original buildings are still standing. One of them is the 1817 adobe church. Other buildings have been rebuilt.

An engraving from the early 1900s shows the ruined church at Mission La Purísima.

Visitors can attend services and admire some of the church's fine murals. They can also tour a museum.

LA PURÍSIMA

La Purísima got help from the U.S. government. In 1934, many men did not have jobs. The government hired some of them to rebuild the mission. Very little of the mission was still standing. Workers made adobe bricks and clay tiles just as the neophytes had. Two hundred men worked for more than seven years. They re-created six of the main mission buildings.

In 1941, La Purísima opened to the public. It is a state historical monument. Since then, workers have rebuilt the rest of the buildings. The mission looks much as it did long ago.

Visitors can see how the neophytes lived and worked. Volunteers weave cloth, as the neophytes did. They also make pottery, soap, and candles. Others work in the fields.

Without a doubt, the missions caused huge changes in the lives of the Chumash and other Native Americans. However, a few miles

Volunteers use the pottery shop at Mission La Purísima to teach about neophytes' work.

Modern Chumash carry on their culture.

from Santa Inés, Chumash culture lives on. The U.S. government set aside the Santa Ynez Reservation for Chumash people. The people who choose to live there have their own government. They run their own businesses. They hold on to Chumash culture. They tell stories, make music, and practice traditional crafts. Together, the people of the Santa Ynez Reservation and the central coast's mission sites tell the varied history of the area and the people who lived there.

LAYOUTS

These diagrams of California's central coast missions show what the missions look like in modern times. Modern-day missions may not look exactly like the original missions Spanish priests founded. But by studying them, we can get a sense of how neophytes and missionaries lived.

Santa Bárbara: Missionaries at Santa Bárbara, founded in 1786, used glass beads, tools, and blankets to encourage the Chumash to build the mission and to be baptized.

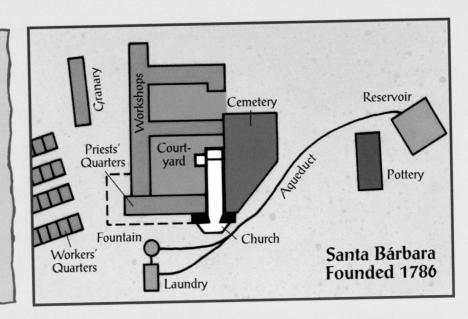

Granary

Workshops

Cemetery

Reservoir

Priests' Quarters

Court-yard

Aqueduct

Pottery

Fountain

Church

Workers' Quarters

Laundry

Santa Bárbara Founded 1786

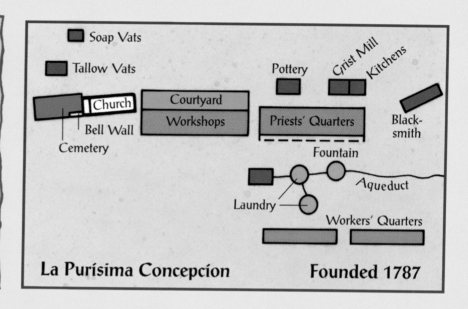

La Purísima Concepción: La Purísima Concepción, founded in 1787, was rebuilt at a different spot in 1813 after earthquakes and floods destroyed the original site.

Soap Vats

Tallow Vats

Church

Bell Wall

Cemetery

Courtyard

Workshops

Pottery

Grist Mill

Kitchens

Priests' Quarters

Black-smith

Fountain

Aqueduct

Laundry

Workers' Quarters

La Purísima Concepción

Founded 1787

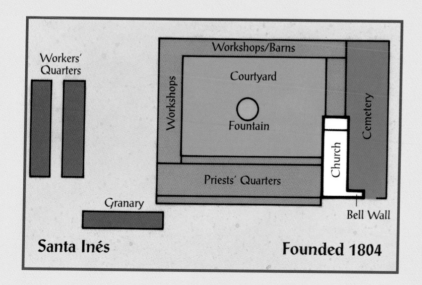

Workers' Quarters

Workshops/Barns

Courtyard

Workshops

Fountain

Cemetery

Church

Priests' Quarters

Granary

Bell Wall

Santa Inés

Founded 1804

Santa Inés: One year after its founding in 1804, Mission Santa Inés didn't have enough workers to succeed. Most of the Native Americans in the area had remained in their villages.

TIMELINE

1769 Father Junípero Serra blesses the site of the first California mission, San Diego de Alcalá.

1786 Mission Santa Bárbara Virgen y Mártir is founded.

1787 Mission La Purísima Concepción de Maria Santísima is founded.

1804 Mission Santa Inés Virgen y Mártir is founded.

1810 New Spain goes to war with Spain.

1821 New Spain wins its independence and becomes the Republic of Mexico.

1824 Chumash revolts occur at all three central coast missions.

1830s The Mexican government secularizes the missions.

1846 The United States declares war on Mexico.

1848 The United States wins the war and takes control of California.

1850 California becomes the thirty-first state.

1850s The U.S. government returns the missions to the Catholic Church. Mission buildings are falling apart.

1880s Mission restorations begin and continue to the present.

GLOSSARY

adobe: bricks made by mixing clay soil with sand, water, and straw

borders: invisible lines that divide one country or region from another

Californios: settlers from Spain or New Spain who made their home in California

drought: a long period of time with little or no rain

missionaries: teachers sent out by religious groups to spread their religion to others

missions: centers where religious people work to spread their faith to others

murals: paintings made directly on a wall

neophytes: Native Americans who have joined the Roman Catholic faith and community

New Spain: modern-day Mexico

presidios: Spanish forts for housing soldiers

pueblos: towns

quadrangle: an area or patio surrounded by buildings on four sides

reservations: pieces of land that have been reserved, or set aside, for use only by Native Americans

restore: to bring something back to its original appearance

revolt: an event in which people act violently to rebel against their government

secularization: to transfer from religious to nonreligious control

PRONUNCIATION GUIDE*

Cabrillo, Juan Rodríguez	kah-BREE-yoh, WAHN roh-DREE-gays
Chumash	CHOO-mash
El Camino Reál	el kah-MEE-noh ray-AHL
La Purísima Concepción de Maria Santísima	lah poo-REE-see-mah con-thep-thee-OHN day mah-REE-ah sahn-TEE-see-mah
Lasuén, Fermín Francisco de	lah-soo-AYN, fair-MEEN frahn-SEES-koh day
Portolá, Gaspar de	por-toh-LAH, gahs-PAHR day
Sagimomatsse, Andrés	sah-hee-moh-MAHTZ, ahn-DRAYS
Santa Bárbara Virgen y Mártir	SAHN-tah BAHR-bahr-ah veer-HAYN ee MAHR-teer
Serra, Junípero	SHE-rrah, hoo-NEE-pay-roh
Tápis, Estéban	TAH-pees, ehs-TAY-bahn
Vizcaíno, Sebastián	vees-kah-EE-noh, say-bahs-tee-AHN

*Local pronunciations may differ.

TO LEARN MORE

Lemke, Nancy. *Southern Coast Missions in California*. Minneapolis: Lerner Publications Company, 2008. Learn all about the missions of California's southern coast.

Nelson, Libby. *California Mission Projects and Layouts*. Minneapolis: Lerner Publications Company, 2008. This book provides guides for building mission models. It also offers layouts of California's twenty-one missions.

Resources for the Mission Santa Ines
http://www.classbrain.com/artmission/publish/article_51.shtml
Learn about the mission's history and explore mussion life then and now.

Santa Barbara Mission
http://www.santabarbara.com/points_of_interest/mission/
Take a virtual tour of this beautiful mission.

Sonneborn, Liz. *The Chumash*. Minneapolis: Lerner Publications Company, 2007. This book introduces the Chumash, Native Americans whose homeland is in California.

Van Steenwyk, Elizabeth. *The California Missions*. New York: Franklin Watts, 1995. Van Steenwyk introduces California missions through clear text and full-color photographs.

Welcome to La Purísima Mission State Historic Park
http://www.lapurisimamission.org
Visit the fourth-grade section of this site to tour the mission and learn about its history. Tour the padre's residence, the kitchens, pottery shop, blacksmith shop, the old infirmary, the main church, the soldiers' quarters, and more.

INDEX